W9-CAZ-704

394.2
B

c. 1

Buell, Hall

Festivals of Japan

394.2
B

c. 1

Buell, Hall

Festivals of Japan

DATE DUE	BORROWER'S NAME	ROOM NUMBER
	KELLY MC	K
	Gary Rodenbaugh	2 11
	Willi	

FESTIVALS OF JAPAN

FESTIVALS OF JAPAN

Hal Buell

ILLUSTRATED WITH PHOTOGRAPHS

DODD, MEAD & COMPANY   New York

✿ For RIKAKO

PHOTOGRAPH CREDITS

Hal Buell—p. 10, 29, 30, 39, 49, 50, 54, 55, 60, 61, 62, 73, 74, 75
M. Mizukami—p. 64, 65
M. Takahara—p. 2, 13, 14, 15, 16, 18, 19, 20, 21, 23, 24, 25, 26, 32, 37, 40, 68,
    69, 70, 71, 77, 78
Japan Tourist Association—p. 27 (top), 34, 38, 43, 44, 45, 51, 52, 53, 57, 58, 66
Japan Travel Bureau—p. 27 (bottom), 33, 35, 42, 48

Copyright © 1965 by Harold G. Buell
All rights reserved
No part of this book may be reproduced in any form
without permission in writing from the publisher
Library of Congress Catalog Card Number: 65-18534
Printed in the United States of America

CONTENTS

THE FESTIVALS OF JAPAN

Japan is a land of festivals.

Every corner of this island country, no matter how remote, celebrates festivals—holidays and special occasions of many kinds. There are religious ceremonies, historical celebrations, holidays just for children, events involving athletic skill, and even Japanese "rodeos."

The Japanese word for festival is *matsuri*, and so that word appears over and over again in this book. The Japanese people love to take part in their *matsuri*. They look forward to them, just as you anticipate the coming of Halloween or Christmas.

Every nation has its special holidays and feast days and patriotic celebrations, each of which tells us something about the country. In America, we have Thanksgiving, a holiday that reminds us of the early settlers who came to the New World and were grateful for the bountiful harvest the land gave them. We have Christmas and Easter, whose origins go back nearly two thousand years to the time of Christ. There is the Fourth of July, when America's independence and love of liberty are remembered, Washington's birthday and Labor Day, and special days that are holidays in only a certain area or in only one of the states.

It is much the same in other countries. Some holidays are celebrated in many lands—Christmas is found around the world, and the Jewish holy day, Yom Kippur, is observed wherever Jewish people are found. But there are festivals that belong to a particular country, too. The French celebrate Bastille Day on July 14 with patriotic displays of their own. May Day is a day of celebration in the Soviet Union. In Canada, Victoria Day and the Queen's Birthday are occasions for festive gatherings, and in England, you would celebrate Boxing Day as a special holiday. Colorful *fiestas* and religious festivals dot the calendar in Spain. In Italy, the Italians observe many saints' days, as well as special festivals like the famous Palio with its horse race and costumes and ceremonies that date back to medieval times.

And so it is in Japan. It is a small country—smaller than the American state of California—with about 100 million people living on its four main islands and the many smaller islands. But it is a land of many festivals—many more than in the United States—and the Japanese delight in spending much time and money on them. Some of the festivals are similar to those in America and other countries, and others are quite different. Some are observed only in the cities, others are held only in rural areas, and some are found only in a particular neighborhood of a city or town. But each month, all across the tiny country, there are countless *matsuri* celebrated with great enthusiasm and excitement, with brightly colored robes and costumes, with flowers, paper dragons, kites, and swords.

The Japanese festivals, like those elsewhere, have their origins in historical events, in the religion of the people, and in the legends of the land.

First, there is the religion of the people. The Christian world observes religious holidays when they observe Christmas and Easter or the special days of the saints. In Asia, however, Buddhism is the main religion. It teaches that life is full of suffering and that self-study will bring enlightenment. The Japanese also practice Shinto-ism, which believes in the basic goodness of mankind and also in ancestor worship. Many Japanese are both Buddhist and Shintoist, and many of their festivals are closely connected to these two religions.

Secondly, many Japanese festivals have their origins far back in the nation's history. In America, our Independence Day on the Fourth of July recreates a part of our American history. In Japan, history is also recreated in holiday celebrations, much more so than in the United States, for Japanese history goes back many more hundreds of years. Japan was once governed by *shoguns,* or war lords, who held the Emperor prisoner and ruled the land in his name. In their courts, the *shoguns* had knights, called *samurai.* The adventures of the *shoguns* and their *samurai* are often played out in colorful modern festivals.

Then there are festivals that have grown out of the country's legends. Some are pure fairy tales, and the modern festivals are merely opportunities for fun and relaxation. Others are stories of the nation's ancient gods. The Japanese were once worshippers of a sun goddess, who had many brothers and sisters. Each god or goddess had a story, and each story was told or acted out in a *matsuri.* Those same stories are remembered in festivals held today.

As you might expect, some of the present-day *matsuri* have stories that combine all three things—religion, history, and legend.

In modern Japan the festivals are sometimes very commercial, designed to draw visitors and business to a particular city or neigh-borhood. Some are so elaborate that tourists come from far places just to see them. Others are social occasions for the people, and still others retain the deep meaning of the past and express the cultural heritage of the Japanese people.

As you will see, some of these Japanese *matsuri* are very like the holidays of the Western world, while others seem strange and very different. But each one tells us something about Japan and the Japanese people.

Chanting and singing, young men carry a portable shrine through a Tokyo street. They wear the colorful jackets of festival participants. A lantern hangs in front of a house as part of the neighborhood *matsuri*.

MATSURI
The Neighborhood Festival

The most popular of all Japanese festivals is called simply *matsuri*, or festival. These festivals, which celebrate the special day of the *ujikami*, or neighborhood god, are similar in their origins to festivals marking the days of special saints in the Western world.

In America, St. Patrick's Day is a carefree holiday celebrated in honor of Ireland's patron saint. And in many Italian communities the people carry huge statues of saints through the streets on the saint's special day.

The big difference in Japan is that a great many more of these festivals are held. Each neighborhood has its own shrine for its own *ujikami*, and most shrines have a special *matsuri* in honor of that particular god.

Some neighborhood *matsuri* are deeply religious, but today most are opportunities for fun-making and celebration.

An air of festivity marks the days prior to the *matsuri* as stores decorate their entrances with paper lanterns and paper flowers. Little stalls offering toys, trinkets and special foods are set up in the shrine's courtyard.

The most spectacular part of the *matsuri* features the young men of the neighborhood carrying a huge palanquin, or portable shrine, on their shoulders through the streets. Spectators throw water on the men as a warning to keep them from crashing the heavy shrine into shop fronts. Some stores put out food and drink for the shrine bearers to enjoy during a rest.

There was a time when most neighborhood *matsuri* were held at night because it was believed the new day started after the evening meal. And what better way to start a new day than by honoring the gods? Later, however, the festivals were held in the daylight hours so that women and children could more conveniently participate.

Recently special *matsuri* have developed. One is marked by the fact that only women carry the shrine. Another features only very young children, carrying a paper shrine.

But despite the various specific meanings, both the city and rural people of Japan dearly love their own local *matsuri* that honor their very own neighborhood gods.

In a special *matsuri*, women carry a heavy shrine through the streets of Yokohama. Male companions, who will take over when the women get tired, watch with smiles on their faces.

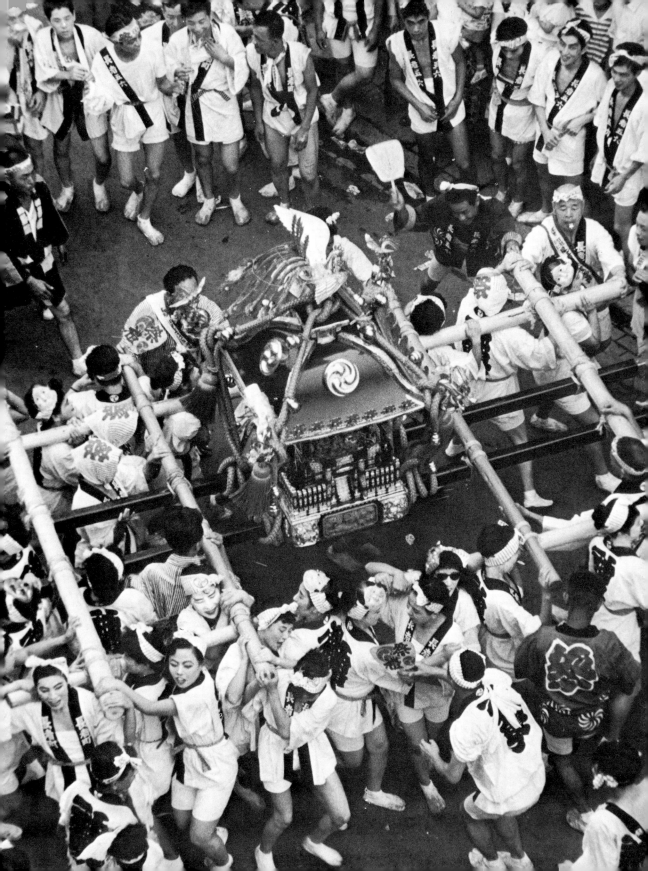

Young boys, carrying a small portable shrine, leave the courtyard of a shrine in Tokyo. A Buddhist monk, right, guides them.
The shrine, built of heavy wooden beams, and plated with gold, is
a heavy load for the youngsters. They strain under its weight.

Time out from a *matsuri* for an ice cream bar.

HANA MATSURI
The Birth of Buddha

Like most people of the Far East, the Japanese accept the teachings of Buddha as their religion. In many ways they feel toward Buddha the same way Western people feel toward Christ. It is no surprise then that the birth of Buddha is widely observed in Japan, as is the birth of Christ in the West.

The anniversary of Buddha's birth comes on April 8. Those who visit a shrine on Buddha's birthday bring flowers—the fresh flowers of spring. And so the festival is called Hana Matsuri, or Flower Festival. It has been observed for more than 1,300 years, dating back to A.D. 606.

In Yokohama, one of Japan's major cities, a great procession is held on April 8. Children, dressed in special *kimono*, march through the streets to the shrine. Students wear robes and sing Buddhist chants. Many people, especially the women and children, carry flower petals to offer to Buddha.

There are even floats. One of them is always a huge white elephant bearing a small image of Buddha. There are no elephants in Japan, but in India, where Buddha spent most of his life, the elephant is common and so the Japanese honor him by having an elephant at his birthday *matsuri*.

Japanese children, wearing special headdress and carrying offerings of flowers, parade through Yokohama, one of Japan's major cities. They are going to visit a Buddhist temple on Buddha's birthday.

Great floats are part of the parade. Students kneel in prayer as a white elephant, made of wire and cloth, passes by. On the elephant's back is a small shrine carrying an image of the infant Buddha.

A little girl, her face powdered white so she will appear clean and fresh to Buddha, pauses during the parade.

Inside the temple shrine, a girl in magnificent robes and elaborate headdress performs a sacred Buddhist rite.

At the shrine, students
in special robes and stock-
inged feet carry offerings
to Buddha as they chant
Buddhist prayers.

NOMAOI MATSURI and YABUSAME
Japanese Rodeos

Not all Japanese *matsuri* have their origins in religious events. Some are buried deep in Japanese history—a history that is not unlike that of countries in the Western world.

English legends are filled with tales of the Knights of the Round Table and their deeds of chivalry. And in America, the cowboy riding his horse across the great plains of the West is an ever-popular hero who is known and admired by young and old.

Tales from Japan's history are similar, but the hero is the *samurai*—a sort of soldier-cowboy-knight—who was armed with a long sword. He lived by a code of loyalty and honor, fought for his leader, and helped the poor. He rode a horse and, as in America and England, good horsemanship was the hallmark of a hero.

Thus it is that one of Japan's most exciting summer festivals is the Wild Horse Festival, or Nomaoi Matsuri, observed on the northeastern plains of Honshu. It is a sort of Japanese rodeo.

Each summer the local townspeople dress up in uniforms common to the *samurai* of centuries ago. They equip their horses with all the trappings of ancient Japan. There follows a thrilling display of horsemanship that lasts three days. Some of the sports include the throwing of banners in the air, to be caught by riders racing their mounts across the plain. On the final day of the festival the riders chase a group of horses into an enclosure where they are captured by other participants with their bare hands.

Another festival, whose origins are lost in history, is Yabusame, or "shooting arrows from a running horse." This festival goes back to the eleventh century when a bow and arrow was the most important weapon.

In the twentieth century, the festival features horsemen, dressed in ancient *samurai* costume, racing their mounts down a stretch of track more than 200 yards long. They shoot at three targets as they charge by, and are scored on their accuracy and horsemanship.

Above, participants in the Wild Horse Festival ride their mounts
to the area of the Nomaoi Matsuri. The riders are dressed in the
ancient garb of the *samurai*.

Still wearing the arm protector and breastplate that are part of the armor of the *samurai*, this man pauses to eat rice during the day's activities.

The young *samurai* across the page finds it difficult to smile. Maybe all that armor is too heavy for comfort.

A mounted *samurai* sits at attention.

Archers of ancient Japan come alive as participants prepare their horses for a run past the target during the Yabusame festival held near Tokyo.

One of them lets fly with an arrow as his horse charges down the track.

THE DANCE OF THE GOLDEN DRAGON
A Special Matsuri

Sometimes a religious shrine will hold a *matsuri* and the men taking part will carry an object through the streets—but not a palanquin.

So it is with the Asakusa Kannon Shrine in Tokyo.

This shrine is best known because it is the place where, 1,200 years ago, two fishermen found a huge wooden image of Kannon, the Buddhist Goddess of Peace. The image was enshrined in a temple in the area of the present Asakusa Shrine. Each day an endless stream of visitors comes to the shrine to pray for peace and prosperity in their families.

And twice each year the Dance of the Golden Dragon—the dragon that guards the spirit of Kannon—is held in the area near the shrine.

The dragon, carried on poles by young men, twists and winds through the streets of the Asakusa neighborhood. Music is played on Japanese instruments by women riding in a small cart.

Children participate in the festival, too. Some carry poles with bells on them and keep time to the music by striking the poles on the ground.

The great Golden Dragon of the Asakusa Kannon Shrine is carried on poles in the courtyard of the shrine in Tokyo. It twists and weaves amid the incense smoke and crowds of people.

The dragon's head takes a rest in a street of Tokyo during one of its two yearly appearances outside the shrine.

Young boys march ahead of the twisting dragon during the Dance of the Golden Dragon. Their poles bear little bells, and they keep the beat of the music of the procession as they march along.

NIKKO GRAND FESTIVAL
The March of the Samurai

The day of the *samurai* in Japanese history was a period of glory and splendor, of brave knights and great loyalties.

The *samurai* reached his greatest position of power when Japan was ruled by Ieyasu Tokugawa, who died about 350 years ago.

For more than 200 years after Tokugawa's death, the military-like *samurai* ruled supreme. He was all things to all men, a knight of unquestioned authority and daring.

To commemorate that period of history the people of Nikko, a city near Tokyo, hold a festival twice each year. The festival, one of Japan's most spectacular, recreates the scene that took place when Tokugawa's remains were transferred from their resting place to the great shrine at Nikko.

On the day of the festival the townspeople dress in their ancient costumes and parade—a thousand strong—up the side of a mountain to the shrine. In addition to *samurai*, there are men in the dress of artisans, storekeepers and performers of the long-ago era.

A huge palanquin, said to carry the spirit of Tokugawa, is carried in the procession on the shoulders of young men, along with other palanquins carrying the spirits of other notable *samurai*.

The glittering, golden, portable shrine and the heavily armored *samurai* warriors who escort it provide a picturesque spectacle in the thickly wooded, mountain surroundings of Nikko.

This festival is so well known that many tourists come to Japan just to see it.

Here the men of Nikko carry portable shrines on their shoulders through the wooded area leading to Toshogu Shrine. The main palanquin is believed to carry the spirit of one of Japan's greatest rulers, Ieyasu Tokugawa.

Two *samurai* of Nikko

A great stone lantern stands like a sentinel as a palanquin is carried by at Nikko.

Dressed as ancient *samurai* and numbering a thousand
strong, marchers parade down the roadway at Toshogu
Shrine. They wear the helmets and armor of Japan's
Tokugawa era.

GION MATSURI
The Gods Stop a Plague

One of Japan's most spectacular festivals dates back to the tenth century—to a time when a terrible plague gripped the land.

It was believed that a brother of Japan's Sun Goddess lived in Yasaka Shrine, in Kyoto, which was then the capital city of Japan.

This spirit possessed the special powers needed to combat the plague. So the young men of Kyoto carried palanquins—with the spirit inside—through the streets of the city.

Sure enough, the legend says, the plague disappeared immediately, and ever since, Kyoto has honored Yasaka Shrine (which was called Gion Shrine a thousand years ago) with a summer *matsuri*.

Twenty huge floats, some that are four stories high, are pulled through the streets by the men of Kyoto. Each float is a work of art in itself. To add splendor, the floats are decorated with rich silks and gold ornaments, and with treasures imported from Europe over the centuries.

In the twentieth century, the Gion Festival, as it is now called, attracts many tourists to Japan. Held in mid-summer, the festival lasts nearly a month, but the floats are pulled through the streets on only two days during July.

Here you can see the long line of men required to pull just one of the great floats through the streets of Kyoto during the Gion Matsuri. Notice the heavy rope needed to move the huge decorated structure that towers far above their heads.

Many of the Gion floats are several stories high. People ride in them, and on top of them, during the festival's procession.

The floats are each a work of art, their sides decorated with
beautiful paintings and pictures woven in cloth.

At night, paper lanterns create a fantastic scene in Kyoto's streets during the Gion Festival.

AOI MATSURI
The Emperor Pays Homage

Hundreds of years ago the Emperor and Empress of Japan, who then lived in Kyoto, would leave their Imperial Palace once each year to pay homage at two shrines in that city.

The custom was called Aoi because part of the ritual consisted of offering leaves of the aoi tree to the gods.

Today this ancient procession is recreated. As in olden times, an oxen pulls an Imperial chariot through the streets of Kyoto, starting at the Imperial Palace and traveling to two of the city's many shrines.

The chariot is accompanied by men and women dressed in the costumes of Japan's old Imperial Court. Some men, representing the police of ancient Kyoto, ride on horseback. Others carry standards, or flags, of the Emperor.

One of Kyoto's most beautiful girls is selected each year to take the same role as that taken by the Emperor's daughter hundreds of years ago. Carried in a decorated palanquin, she is part of the elaborate procession.

At the shrines, Shinto priests perform sacred ceremonies before the chariot, and then it returns to the palace.

In his fancy headdress and carrying a wooden paddle, this man plays the part of a court official during the ceremonies of the festival.

Dressed in the court costume of ancient Japan, men guide an ox-drawn chariot through Kyoto's streets as they observe Aoi Matsuri in the old Japanese capital.

A beautiful girl is chosen to represent the Emperor's daughter who accompanied her parents to the shrines. Here she is carried on the shoulders of men during the Aoi Matsuri parade.

Attired as men and women of the Emperor's court, the procession makes its way through the streets, portraying a scene from Japan's history that took place centuries ago.

After its trip from Kyoto's Imperial Palace, the chariot pulled by an oxen arrives at the shrine.

FESTIVALS FOR CHILDREN
Shichi-Go-San, Children's Day, and Hina-Matsuri

The Japanese people have a deep love for children, and several festivals of Japan are devoted exclusively to boys and girls. The most popular one is Shichi-Go-San, or Seven-Five-Three.

On this day, in mid-November, children of seven, five and three years of age are dressed in their best clothes. (Sometimes special clothes are rented for the occasion.) With the girls' faces powdered a dead white, the children are taken to visit nearby shrines where parents offer thanks for past benefits and pray for the continued growth and development of their youngsters.

Children of three years are included in the festival because that is the year the Japanese consider them to have outgrown babyhood. More than a century ago, the five-year-old group included only boys. It was the occasion when they met their feudal lord and only boys were allowed this honor. And at that time only seven-year-old girls marked the day because that was when little girls began wearing full *kimono* with the classical *obi*, or belt, thus taking the first step toward womanhood.

Today, however, both boys and girls of seven, five and three years participate in the festival. After a visit to the shrine, the parents hold a party in their home. The children receive gifts from relatives, neighbors and friends.

Another popular festival is Children's Day. The purpose of this festival is to impress upon the youngsters the importance of being good citizens, to have courage and to be strong in the face of danger.

This holiday was once known as Boys' Day, and only male children were honored. But in later years the festival was expanded to include girls also. However, the emphasis is still primarily on boys. Parents who have sons erect a flagpole outside their house, and huge paper and cloth replicas of carp are flown from the top. To the Japanese, the carp is a symbol of strength and courage, qualities that Japanese parents hope to see in their sons.

Inside the houses, exhibits of ancient *samurai* armor, battle flags of ancient Japan, and models of centuries-old weapons are put on display.

The girls have a special day, too. It's called Hina-Matsuri, the Doll Festival. The origins of this festival are lost in history. But celebrations now are marked by the display of dolls—always two main dolls, a man and a woman representing the Emperor and Empress—on a huge platform in the household.

Little girls, dressed in their best *kimono*, invite their friends to their home where they eat sweetcakes made of rice, and drink a very mild rice wine.

Department stores in Japan's cities have special doll fairs during the weeks prior to Hina-Matsuri. Magnificent collections of dolls are shown.

Many brides often take their doll collections with them to their new homes after marriage and pass them on to their daughters.

Parents accompany their children to a shrine on Shichi-Go-San (Seven-Five-Three) festival day. The children wear their very best *kimono* on this day, or formal Western clothes. The parents offer prayers of thanks for the blessings of the past year and pray for the continued growth and happiness of the children in the years to come.

Afterward there is a party at home, with refreshments and gifts to celebrate the important occasion.

A mother adjusts a hair-bow during a Seven-Five-Three festival, but her little girl is more interested in ice cream.

Dressed in the formal *kimono* of a *samurai*, this little boy attends festivities at a Tokyo shrine. He even carries a *samurai* sword.

On Children's Day, cloth and paper carp fly from poles outside
the homes of parents who have sons.

Inside the homes, displays of ancient weapons are put up to inspire the young men to bravery and courage. Shown here are battle flags and arrows. The boy is holding a sword as his mother fits him with the helmet of a *samurai*.

On Hina-Matsuri, the Doll's Festival, little girls wear their holiday *kimono* and enjoy drinks and sweets with friends in their homes. In the background is a display of dolls dressed in the costumes of Japan's ancient Imperial Court.

A Japanese girl, with an elaborate hairbow for Hina-Matsuri, looks at the dolls on display. You can see them, too, across the page. On the top level is the male Emperor doll. With him is the lady doll, the Empress of ancient Japan.

KANTO MATSURI
Harvest Festivals

Almost all nations have festivals or celebrations connected with the planting and harvesting of crops.

Americans have celebrated Thanksgiving Day—the day we offer prayers of thanks for a bountiful harvest—ever since the Pilgrims first came to the New World.

Since rice is the most important of all foods to the Japanese, there are popular festivals held to mark the times of the planting and harvesting of rice.

The primary purpose of these festivals is to ask divine help in the growing of the year's crop. Every year, in mid-August, the people of Akita City hold a special festival to seek the help of the gods for a good harvest.

On this day young men of the area, all clad in picturesque dress, try their skill at balancing long bamboo poles strung with many lanterns on their hands, foreheads, shoulders or hips.

These poles with all the lanterns attached are called *kanto*, and so the festival is called the Kanto Matsuri. The most skillful performers can balance a *kanto* with forty to fifty lanterns. How many can you count in the picture here?

Near Osaka, Japan's second largest city, Buddhist monks give their blessing as the first of the year's crop is put into a rice paddy outside a shrine.

SETSUBUN
Cast Out the Devils

"In with good luck, out with the old demon."

That sounds very much like the saying often heard in America on New Year's Day: "Out with the old, in with the new."

"In with good luck, out with the old demon" is the greeting the Japanese exchange on Setsubun, the celebration that marks the changing of the year.

The festival takes place in February, at a time when, under Japan's old calendar, the seasons changed. In olden days the Japanese believed that the new year started with the change of seasons from winter to spring. Their ancient calendar put this at the first several days of February.

On this festival day the people gather at major shrines where famous persons—athletes, wrestlers, actors, actresses, politicians— throw dried beans at the crowd and shout their good wishes.

The picturesque custom of bean throwing is widely celebrated in Japan. It marks the casting out of the devils that caused the year's bad luck. Each person is supposed to eat one bean for each year since their birth, plus one extra bean for the coming year. Those who catch the beans thrown by the famous persons keep them for the whole year as "good luck" charms.

Inside the shrine, before beans are thrown to the people, the monks give their blessing to the dignitaries who will participate.

After this blessing, the chief monk of the shrine, carrying a box of beans, goes out to throw the first beans to the people.

Then, as a climax to the ceremony, the famous people at the shrine throw beans to the people gathered in the courtyard. Some hold their hats out to catch as many "good luck" beans as possible.

SNOW FESTIVAL
Sculptures Instead of Snowmen

Each year some areas of Japan are subject to heavy snowfall and bitter cold weather, much like the winter weather of Maine or Michigan or Minnesota.

In fact, the snowfall is so great that people must use sleds and skis to travel about.

In Sapporo, the main city of Japan's northernmost island, the Japanese hold a yearly Snow Festival. The most interesting part of this festival is the construction of huge statues, buildings, and scenes from stories or legends. The scenes are built of carefully carved ice and snow.

Foreign tourists and the Japanese themselves travel great distances to see the Snow Festival.

Like children everywhere, the boys and girls of Japan like to play in the snow. In many rural communities they build snow huts, much like Alaskan igloos, and play inside.

These cave-like huts are called *kamakura*. The children leave their shoes outside, just as they do at the entrances of their homes. Inside the snow hut they eat sweets and play games.

The Snow Festival of Sapporo is held right in the heart of the city, where huge crowds gather to see the marvels made of ice and snow.

Each year the festival has a special theme. The sculptures shown here will be familiar to children of Western lands, for the theme is fairy tales. There is Cinderella, with her coach behind her, and the prince's castle in the background.

And the giant figure is Gulliver, of *Gulliver's Travels*.

In some places in Japan children build their own snow buildings, like this hut, which is called a *kamakura*. It's just like a house and, in the Japanese tradition, the youngsters have left their shoes outside.

DEZOME-SHIKI
The Firemen's Parade

Most American boys and girls love to visit the firehouse. They like to see the big trucks, touch the gleaming red metal of the great engine, and ring the bell on its hood.

Japanese youngsters are even fonder of firemen than American children are. The reason is simple. It is because their houses are made of wood and paper, and each year there are several great fires that consume whole neighborhoods in the big cities.

So while Japanese boys and girls like to see the firemen's equipment, just as you do, they also appreciate very much the work they do in protecting their homes. The fireman's bravery in battling the flames makes him a sort of modern *samurai*.

Each year in Tokyo the firemen hold an exciting parade. It is called Dezome-Shiki, and the different fire companies show off all their modern equipment.

But there is a touch of the past, too. The firemen carry the standards, or flags, of their units, wear clothes like those of olden times, and perform daring acrobatic feats atop high ladders. It is a thrilling sight—as breath-taking as any performance at a circus.

The standard, or emblem, of this fire company is twirled during Dezome-Shiki, the annual fireman's parade in Tokyo. But the most spectacular part comes when firemen climb their ladders and perform daring acrobatics high in the sky . . .

. . . and without hands, too.

A fireman and his son await the start of the parade. The colored streamers hanging from this fire company's standard are quiet now, but soon will be twirled about in a dazzling display for Dezome-Shiki.

HARI-KUYO
Final Rest for Broken Needles

Sewing is an important art for all Japanese women. It was so in ancient times and also in the Japan of today.

The modern Japanese woman will likely use a sewing machine. But in olden days, when elaborate *kimono* made of gold and silver thread were popular, needles of all sizes and shapes were common items in all households. In the course of a year's work, many were broken or bent.

Needles were important to Japanese women, who believed, as did their menfolk, that all things contributing to the comfort of human beings should be honored after they outlived their usefulness.

And so a festival came into being a hundred years ago called Hari-Kuyo, The Mass of the Broken Needles.

On a day, usually in December, women and young girls bring their broken and bent needles to a local shrine where a special altar is set up. On the altar are placed offerings of food and drink, and also a great container of *tofu*, a soft bean-curd.

The women and girls stick their broken needles into the bean-curd so that the needles that have served them well throughout the year may have a soft rest after their months of hard labor.

As the Mass of the Broken Needles begins, a small shrine bearing a tiny image of Buddha is carried outside to the accompaniment of music.

The girls who participate in the ceremony dress up in their best *kimono*. In some places the festival is held more as a social occasion for the women of the neighborhood, rather than as a religious service. But those who take part still meet at the shrine and leave their broken needles on the altar.

Offerings of food are placed on the altar and young
girls of the neighborhood, dressed in ceremonial robes,
take their place in front of the *tofu*, or bean-curd.

Needles of all sizes and shapes are placed in the soft
tofu. It is their reward for a year of good service.

TANABATA

A Legend of the Heavens

Every summer, on July 7, several of Japan's cities turn into fairylands. In the streets huge streamers of every imaginable color rustle in the wind like a brilliant paper forest.

This festival is called Tanabata, the Festival of the Stars.

The story of the festival is about the love between two stars— the Weaver Princess Star and the Herdboy Star.

The celestial princess, highly skilled in the art of weaving, was the daughter of a heavenly king. She fell in love with the Herdboy Star, a lad of lowly birth. But the king was a kindly man and he allowed them to marry.

So much in love were they, however, that they neglected their duties. The clothes were not woven and the herds strayed across the starry sky.

The king became angry and ruled that the sweethearts must live on opposite sides of the Milky Way, the sparkling river of the heavens. They were to meet on only one night, July 7, the night when the Herdboy Star and the Weaver Princess Star cross in the heavens.

The legend is widely known, and the Japanese observe this festival in a spirit of joy.

Crowds throng the streets of a town near Tokyo during Tanabata, and shopowners and businessmen do a brisk business.

A paper forest of every imaginable color rustles overhead as a policeman directs traffic during Tanabata.

INDEX

About the Author

This is Hal Buell's third photographic book about Japan and Asia for young readers. He is also the photographer-author of YOUNG JAPAN and MAIN STREETS OF SOUTHEAST ASIA.

The author and his family—wife, Angela, and daughter, Barbara, 10—lived in the Orient for four years until 1963. He was assigned there as Asia Photo Editor for The Associated Press and traveled widely in the area from Burma to Japan, and south to Indonesia.

Buell, now Photo Projects Editor for The Associated Press, is based in New York, and covers assignments both in the United States and abroad.

The Buells live in Westchester County, north of New York City, where Mrs. Buell is a teacher and their daughter attends school. The author, now thirty-three years old, is a graduate of Northwestern University's Medill School of Journalism.